lost

D0382375

Flying Eagle

Sudipta Bardhan-Quallen

Illustrated by Deborah Kogan Ray

San Diego Public Library
LOGAN

Charlesbridge

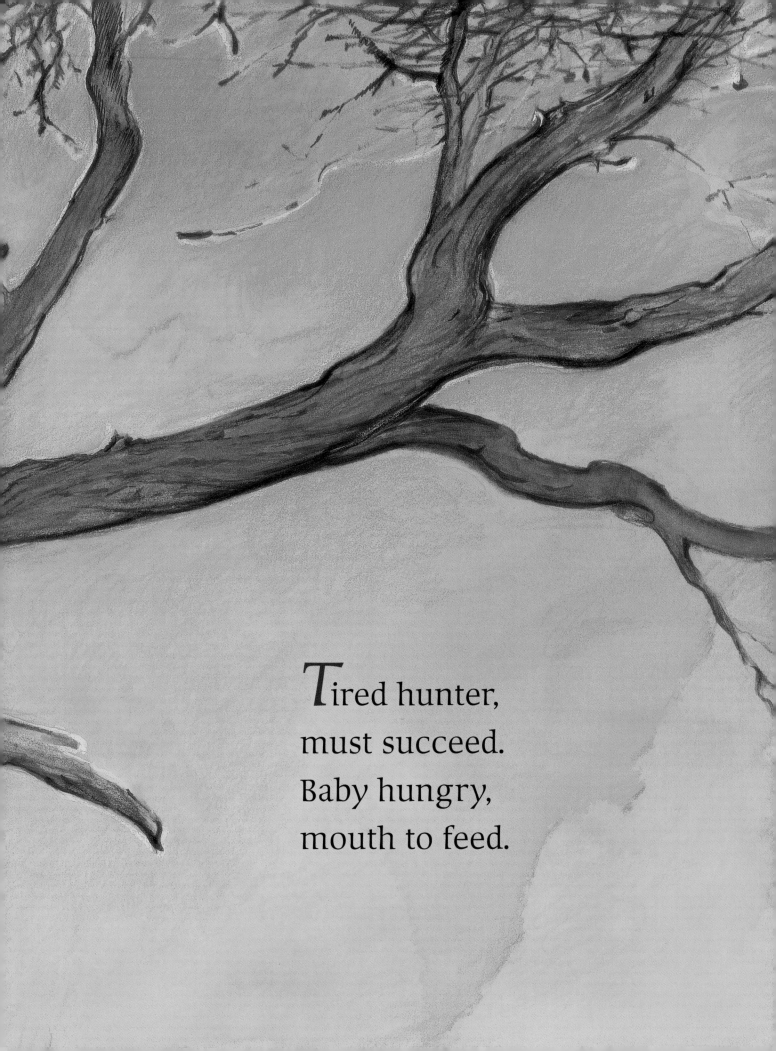

Tired hunter,
must succeed.
Baby hungry,
mouth to feed.

Flying eagle,
soaring high.
Blazing sunset,
crimson sky.

Hippos lounge
by crocodiles.
Lazy giants,
toothy smiles.

Spitting cobra
slithers, slides.
Eagle diving,
cobra hides.

Scanning, seeking,
east and west.
Hunt continues,
cannot rest.

Roaring lions
prowl below.
Tracking, stalking,
growling low.

Lion watches—
then attacks!
Zebras gallop,
zigzag pack.

In the grassland,
herd of gnu.
Grazing rhinos,
two by two.

Dik-diks feeding
in a group.
Eagle spies them,
speedy swoop.

Dik-diks scurry,
one by one.
Eagle's dinner
on the run.

Eagle drawing
near the ground.
Bowstring quivers,
sudden sound.

Poacher's arrow,
lightning fast.
Eagle dodges,
skirting past.

Sky has darkened.
Hard to see.
Stop and perch
atop a tree.

By the water,
something's there—
softly drinking,
little hare.
Eagle plunges,
hare is quick.
Empty talons,
reeds too thick.

Tired, weary,
flying low.
Must find dinner,
far to go.

Soaring over
kudu herd.
Unexpected
weaver bird.
Chasing, trailing,
frantic flight.
Zigging, zagging,
through the night.

Feathers flurry,
tumble, fall.
Talons clutching,
gleeful call.

Sun has vanished,
sky is black.
Chirping baby,
father's back.

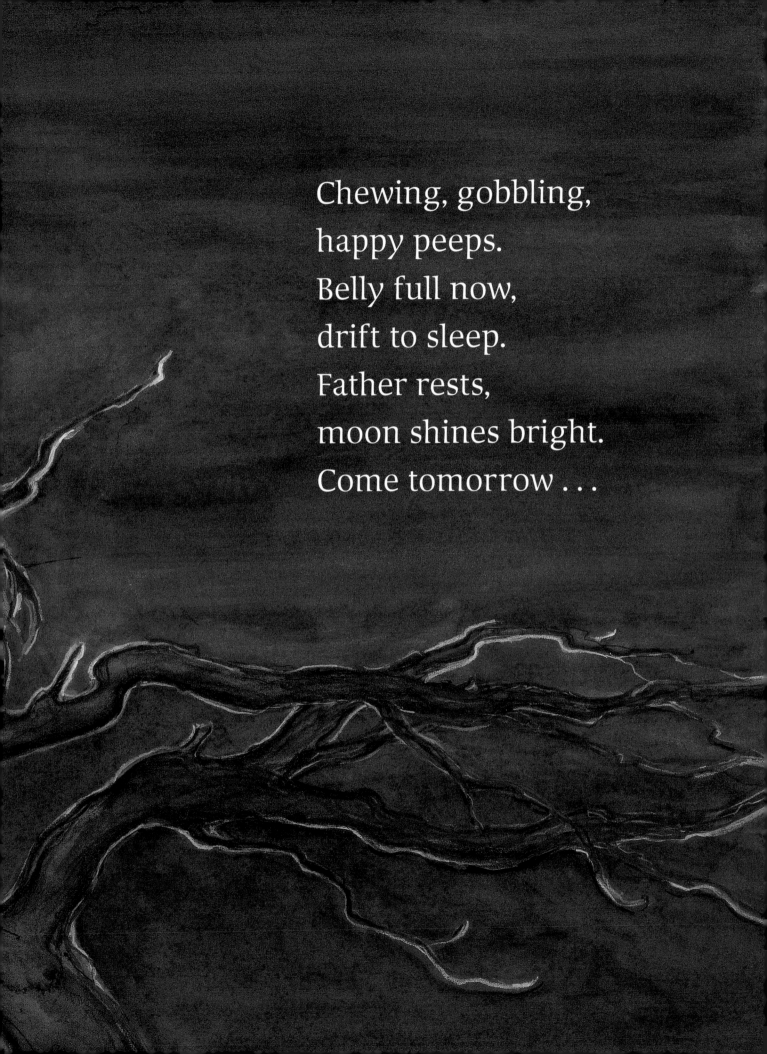

Chewing, gobbling,
happy peeps.
Belly full now,
drift to sleep.
Father rests,
moon shines bright.
Come tomorrow . . .

. . . another flight.

A Majestic Eagle

The tawny eagle is one of the world's most majestic birds of prey. After the martial eagle and the crowned hawk-eagle, it is the largest bird of prey in Africa. Tawny eagles are often found flying over Serengeti National Park, a wildlife refuge in the African country of Tanzania. They hunt everything from insects and reptiles to other birds and small mammals.

Tawny eagle hatchlings are cared for by both parents. Clutches consist of three eggs, but only one chick survives. The oldest chick usually kills off any younger siblings in the nest. By doing this the chick increases its chances of survival. Both parents hunt, but most often it is the father that brings food to the chick. Tawny eagles are diurnal, which means they are active during the day. They prefer to hunt when the sun is out so they can use their powerful vision to search for prey. However, a tawny eagle will search for food as long as it takes, especially when there is a baby to feed. Sometimes a hunt can last long into the night.

Serengeti National Park

Serengeti National Park, located on the Serengeti Plain, extends over five thousand square miles. The word *Serengeti* comes from the Maasai language and means "extended place." The land is very diverse, with grassy plains, savannas, woodlands, and clay plains. Over five hundred different types of animals live there, including the tawny eagle and its prey.

Many of the Serengeti's animals are in danger from poachers—people who illegally hunt animals. Poachers will hunt almost any animal and often do not care how many animals get hurt. Poaching is illegal, so poachers sneak into wildlife preserves after dark to hunt. They often use bows and arrows and snares—weapons that kill silently. Though governments and wildlife preservation societies do much to prevent poaching, it is still a great risk to all animals.

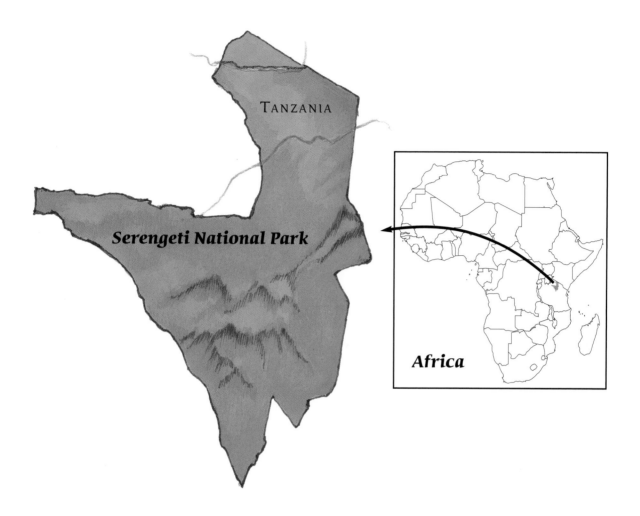

Tanzania

Serengeti National Park

Africa

The Serengeti Plain at Night

In many ways the Serengeti comes to life after the sun goes down. While zebras, gnu, and many other animals search for a safe place to spend the night, a whole new crowd of animals begins their day. Predators like lions, leopards, and crocodiles emerge to find dinner. Darkness allows these predators to sneak up on their prey more easily. Other animals, like hippopotamuses, come out at night to graze. At night they do not have to worry about the hot African sun drying out their sensitive skin.

By morning, animals that hunted or ate all night go to sleep, and those that survived the night wake up. No matter what time it is, the Serengeti is always full of wildlife.

Resources

The Hawk Conservancy Trust—Tawny Eagle
www.hawk-conservancy.org/priors/frodo.shtml
The Hawk Conservancy Trust works to save endangered raptors. Learn more about this bird of prey.

Iwago, Mitsuaki. *Serengeti: Natural Order on the African Plain*. San Francisco: Chronicle Books, 1986.

Peters, Lisa Westberg. *Serengeti*. New York: Crestwood House, 1989.

Parry-Jones, Jemima. *Eagle and Birds of Prey*. New York: Dorling Kindersley, 2000.

Serengeti—The National Park's Official Site
http://www.serengeti.org
Learn more about wildlife, conservation, research, and history.

Tanzania Tourist Board :: Places to Go :: National Parks & Reserves :: Serengeti
http://tanzaniatouristboard.com/places_to_go/national_parks_and_reserves/serengeti
Discover more about the Serengeti National Park from the Tanzania Tourist Board.

To Sawyer
        —S. B.

To Naomi
        —D. K. R.

Text copyright © 2009 by Sudipta Bardhan-Quallen
Illustrations copyright © 2009 by Deborah Kogan Ray
All rights reserved, including the right of reproduction in whole or in part in any form.
Charlesbridge and colophon are registered trademarks of Charlesbridge Publishing, Inc.

Published by Charlesbridge
85 Main Street
Watertown, MA 02472
(617) 926-0329
www.charlesbridge.com

Library of Congress Cataloging-in-Publication Data
Bardhan-Quallen, Sudipta.
    Flying eagle / Sudipta Bardhan-Quallen ; illustrated by Deborah Kogan Ray.
        p. cm.
    ISBN 978-1-57091-671-7 (reinforced for library use)
1. Tawny eagle—Juvenile literature. I. Ray, Deborah Kogan, 1940– ill. II. Title.
QL696.F32.B362 2009
598.9'42—dc22   2007017186

Printed in China
(hc) 10 9 8 7 6 5 4 3 2 1

Illustrations done in watercolor and colored pencil on 140-lb. Arches hot-press watercolor paper
Display type and text type set in NeueNeuland TF and Sierra
Color separations by Chroma Graphics, Singapore
Printed and bound by Jade Productions
Production supervision by Brian G. Walker
Designed by Diane M. Earley